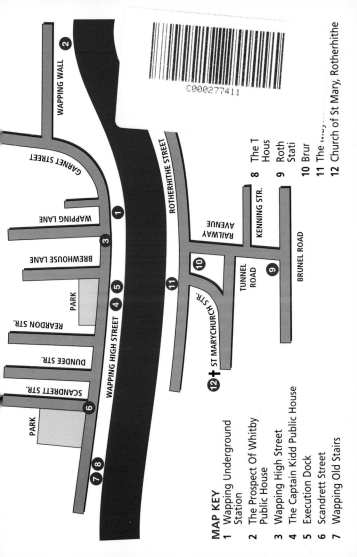

MAP KEY

1 Wapping Underground Station
2 The Prospect Of Whitby Public House
3 Wapping High Street
4 The Captain Kidd Public House
5 Execution Dock
6 Scandrett Street
7 Wapping Old Stairs
8 The T Hous
9 Roth Stati
10 Brur
11 The ...
12 Church of St Mary, Rotherhithe

USEFUL INFORMATION

We recommend that you visit all four Pubs mentioned in this Walk – so the best times to take the Walk (i,e., when all the Pubs are open) are:

- Weekdays between 11.00 am and 11.00 pm
- All day on a Saturday
- Any evening between 5.30 pm and 11.00 pm, except Sundays (when The Mayflower closes early)

Further details about the Pubs:

The Prospect of Whitby: Open seven days a week
from 11.00 am to 11.00 pm
Tel.: 020 7481 1095
Pub food sold in bar all day.
Reservations required for upstairs Restaurant.

The Captain Kidd: Mon. – Sat., 11.00 am to 11.00 pm;
Sun., 12.00 noon to 10.30 pm.
Tel.: 020 7480 5759.

The Town of Ramsgate: Daily, 11.30 am to 11.00 pm .
Tel.: 020 7481 8000
Meals served at lunch and evening times.

The Mayflower: Mon. – Sat., 11.30 am to 11.00 pm;
Sun., 12.00 noon to 3.00 pm only.
Tel.: 020 7237 4088
Upstairs restaurant serves traditional
British dishes.

Church of St Mary Rotherhithe: Daily, 7.30 am to dusk.
Tel.: 020 7231 2465

START OF THE WALK

Directions: *Start the Walk at Wapping Underground Station, which can be reached via the East London Underground Line.*

Exit Wapping Underground Station ❶ *and turn right and walk on the right hand side of the road along Wapping High Street. Continue along as the road curves to the left, past Crane Wharf and turn into the next road on the right, which is called Wapping Wall. Continue along Wapping Wall on the right until you reach The Prospect of Whitby Pub* ❷

The Prospect of Whitby Public House: This famous Pub, which was built in the 1520s, in the reign of King Henry VIII, proclaims itself to be the oldest riverside Inn and has successfully served patrons during the reigns of 22 different Monarchs. There is a list of all 22 monarchs on a board hanging outside the main entrance. This historic Pub still retains its original 400 year-old flagstone floor and boasts a very rare pewter bar-top. The Pub has a small garden terrace which overlooks the Thames and a comfortable Riverside lounge, from where there are good views of the River. Pub food is sold throughout the day in the main bar.

Upstairs, there is a restaurant (open evenings only), in which you can dine overlooking the Thames; Charles Dickens, Princess Margaret, Prince Rainier and Kirk Douglas are among those who have dined here.

The Prospect of Whitby was built in around 1520 and was originally named The Devil's Tavern. As the original name suggests, the Pub had strong associations with sea rovers, sailors, pirates, thieves, smugglers and all types of "low life", who were associated with the River. The Pub also had visits from press gangs in search of crews for ships.

The bodies of drowned men were often found along this stretch of the River. Several of these men had, in fact, been customers of the many nearby Riverside Pubs and inns. The poor men, after drinking too much ale, would be bundled into a small boat and taken out to the centre of the River and thrown overboard to drown. After the victims had drowned, their bodies were retrieved and sold to medical schools and student doctors to be used for study.

During the late 1600s, one frequent visitor at The Prospect of Whitby was the infamous "hanging Judge" Jeffreys, who lived close by in Butchers Row. The Judge became notorious for his brutality and had a liking for executions - he sentenced to hang at least 300 men (and transported at least another 800) after the Monmouth Rebellion in 1685. After condemning the men to death, it is said that the Judge would come here, sit on the rear balcony, and enjoy his lunch while watching the men, whom he had condemned, hang at Execution Dock ❺ The Judge must have been good at his job, because as a reward, King James gave him a peerage. When James II was overthrown in 1688, Judge Jeffreys lost his privileged royal protection and became a wanted man.

Another regular customer at this Pub was Samuel Pepys, the diarist. Pepys was employed as Secretary to the Admiralty, and it is recorded that he often visited the Devil's Tavern when he was in Wapping on naval business. A coastal chart, which was presented to Pepys in 1686, is displayed on a wall upstairs, in the Pepys Room, where the diarist himself would often dine. The Pepys Society later regularly met in the Pepys Room.

In the early 1700s, a sailor returning from the West Indies, brought some beautiful flowers into the bar of the Pub. The flowers had not been seen before by the local people and were apparently the first flowers of this type to be found in the country. The sailor sold the flowers, in return for a quarter of a pint of rum, to a local man, who was a market gardener. The gardener produced from this first plant, several hundred more like it. The flower became, and still is extremely popular all over Great Britain and is called the "fuchsia".

Charles Dickens was another regular customer at this Pub and he is also supposed to have dined upstairs. It is believed by some that he used this Pub in the novel "Our Mutual Friend" as a model for the pub called The Six Jolly Fellowship Porters. (However, there is another pub, called The Grapes, further along the River, which also claims to be the model.) It was during the time of Dickens that the Pub's name was changed from The Devil's Tavern to The Prospect of Whitby. The change of name occurred because a ship called "The Prospect", registered at Whitby in England, was moored nearby for several years and the Ship and the Pub became a famous landmark.

Due to the proximity of The Prospect of Whitby to the Thames, it was very popular with artists, including Turner, Whistler and Cox, who were regular customers and particularly liked to paint sunsets over the Thames from the riverside balcony.

As you exit the Pub, there are some steps, called the Pelican Stairs, which lead down to the River bank. Be very careful if you decide to take a closer look at the Thames!

Directions: *Exit the Pub. Turn left and continue along on the left hand side. Continue to the very end; at the junction with Garnet Street turn left. Continue along Wapping High Street and on the left you will arrive at Wapping Underground Station* ❶

Continue past the Underground Station and along Wapping High Street ❸
which continues directly ahead.

Wapping High Street: In the 16th and 17th centuries, there were dozens of pubs along this small stretch of road and probably as many brothels. The area was described by John Stow in 1598 as:

> *"the usual place of execution for the hanging of pirates*
> *and sea rovers, at the water mark, and there to remain,*
> *till three tides had overflowed them."*

and:

> *"a continual street, or filthy straight passage,*
> *with alleys of small tenements, or cottages,*
> *built and inhabited by sailors and victuallers."*

Directions: *Continue along on the left-hand side of Wapping High Street until you arrive at The Captain Kidd Pub* ❹

The Captain Kidd Public House: This is a relatively modern Pub; however, the building is regarded as dating from the 17th century and was originally used by boat builders and sail makers. The Pub has an upstairs restaurant called The Gallows Restaurant, which has wonderful views of the River Thames and London.

Over the centuries, hundreds of pirates and other River criminals, who were sentenced to death, were brought here, to this stretch of the River bank, to be publicly hanged. After the criminals had been hung, their bodies were tied to stakes at the low tide level and left for three tides to wash over them.

As early as the reign of King Henry VI (1422 -1461), it is recorded that two seamen were hanged here, for murdering three Flemish immigrants in a Flemish Vessel and:

> *"there they hengen till the water had washed them by*
> *ebbying and flowyd, so that the water bett upon them."*

The exact number of men executed here is unknown, but the hangings were frequent and often several men were hung at the same time. On Friday, 30th August 1583, it was recorded that there were ten executions of pirates in one day.

In the 1600s, the authorities built a gallows here, at the River's edge, which became known as "Execution Dock".

Traditionally, the condemned man, while standing at the water's edge, was forced into a horse-drawn cart. He would be allowed to make a final speech, in the hope that he would confess his sins and apologise for his mistakes. However, often these men, who were sometimes drunk, would instead abuse the crowd or the King. When the condemned man had finished his speech, a noose would be placed and tightened around his neck and the horse would be whipped, leaving him "dancing the Hempen Jig" - the pirate slang for "being hung".

In 1729, John Gow, alias Captain Smith, and seven others were hung at Execution Dock. Smith's friends, anxious to put him out of his misery as he swung, ran forward to pull his legs (not an uncommon act by a loved one). Unfortunately, they pulled his legs so forcibly that the rope broke. Captain Smith was hung again shortly afterwards.

The exact position of Execution Dock ❺ is uncertain. However, if you stand at the back of The Captain Kidd Pub, looking out over the River Thames, the favourite site for Execution Dock is on the left of the Pub, at the low tide mark, under the jetty, which leads out into the Thames. You will only be able to see this site, on the stony shore of the Thames, if the tide is out. Some people say that, also at low tide, it is still possible to see the remains of the original wooden posts, to which were tied the bodies of the executed criminals, so that they could be washed over three times by the tide.

Executions at Execution Dock always brought out large crowds of people. Mothers, children and entire families would crowd along the River bank, to get a good view and watch the spectacle, which was, at that time, regarded as a form of entertainment.

The last execution here took place on Thursday, 16th December 1830. Two men had been convicted of piracy, after they attempted to escape from

transportation to America by stirring a revolt on board, and temporarily managing to seize, the transport ship "Cypress".

The Captain Kidd Pub is obviously named after one of the most famous pirates who was executed at Execution Dock. Captain Kidd was a notorious sea captain who, in 1696, was commissioned by the Admiralty to catch pirates for the King. However, instead of catching pirates, he began raiding French Ships (England was at war with the French at this time), keeping the gold booty for himself and not giving it back to the aristocrats, who where paying his wages.

Captain Kidd sailed to Boston, USA, where he surrendered on the promise of a pardon in 1699. However, he was then returned to London for trial, where he was sentenced to death. On 23rd May 1701, Kidd was marched through the streets of London to Execution Dock. He was taken down to the River's edge and chained to a post. While waiting for the hangman, he looked up at the large crowd of people on the River bank. Here, he saw an ex-lover laughing at him and he shouted:

> *"I have lain with that bitch three times –*
> *and now she's come to see me hanged."*

It was recorded that Captain Kidd experienced a terrible death - the hangman's rope broke twice, throwing him to the ground, and he was only successfully hung on the third attempt! Kidd's body was immediately dipped in hot tar and left for three tides to wash over him. The body was later taken to Tilbury Point and, as was the case with the bodies of other famous pirates, hung from inside a metal cage for three years as a warning to other pirates.

Directions: Exit the Pub and turn left. Continue along Wapping High Street on the right hand side and turn into the third street on the right, which is called Scandrett Street ❻. (The Street may not be labelled with a road sign, but you should be able to identify it as it runs along the side of a park.)

Notice, on your left hand side, as you walk, a cleared green area called Wapping New Stairs - this is a good place to get another view of the Thames.

Scandrett Street: If you enter Scandrett Street, you will find on your right, St John's of Wapping School; this was founded in 1695 and is today closed and up for sale. St John's Church is nearby; this was converted into flats after the Church was partially demolished in the Blitz during the Second World War.

During the 1700s, Scandrett Street was part of an alley, called Gun Alley, which led down to the River, as Scandrett Street does today. At No. 13 Gun Alley, lived William Peckover, who sailed with Captain Cook on all three of his voyages. In fact, several members of the crews, which Captain Cook used on his voyages, lived locally.

In 1776, Peckover sailed with Cook to discover the north-west passage in The Discovery. It was during this voyage that Peckover became acquainted with William Bligh, who was then aged 21 and was the Master responsible for navigation on the ship, The Resolution, which had sailed with The Discovery. The voyage ended in disaster when natives in Hawaii killed Captain Cook.

In 1787, William Bligh was given command of The Bounty and was sent to Tahiti and Jamaica to collect new varieties of food. Peckover, who was now 40, and suffered from rheumatism, was appointed Gunner and given his own cabin.

After spending five months in Tahiti, it was on the return journey that the crew of The Bounty mutinied. Peckover was set adrift in a launch boat with Captain Bligh and seventeen other men, without a map and 3,600 miles from the nearest European settlement, which was Coupang in Timor. The rations on board were an ounce of bread and a quarter pint of water daily per man. A month later, Bligh and his men reached the Great Barrier Reef and managed to stop on an island to stock up with berries and shellfish. Realising that they would never be rescued from here, they set sail again on starvation rations before eventually reaching Timor.

Of the nineteen men set adrift after the mutiny, eighteen reached Timor safely. William Peckover survived and returned safely home to England and to his family in Gun Alley, Wapping - where he most probably celebrated his safe return at the next ancient Pub we will come to on this Walk - The Town of Ramsgate.

Directions: *Return down Scandrett Street and turn right along Wapping High Street. Shortly on the left, you will come to The Town of Ramsgate Pub* **8**

NB: Before you enter the Pub, notice the passage at the side of the Pub called Wapping Old Stairs **7**

Wapping Old Stairs: One of the few original landing stairs still remaining along this side of the River. At one stage, there were dozens of similar stairs leading down to the River. The stairs were used for landing small boats, which transferred people and goods to the larger ships, which were moored further out in the Thames.

It is claimed, that it was on these steps, that Judge Jeffreys was seized by a mob. The Judge, having lost his royal protection and now a wanted man, was reported to have been recognised having a drink in the bar of The Town of Ramsgate, while waiting for a boat to take him to Europe.

Macaulay describes the incident:

> *"The dress was that of a common sailor,*
> *and was black with coal dusk, but there was no mistaking*
> *the savage eye and mouth".*

Jeffreys was surrounded by the mob, who were howling for revenge, and - terrified - was taken to the Tower of London, where he eventually died, years later, not due to violence or the effects of his incarceration, but from drinking too much alcohol! He is considered:

> *"the worst Judge that ever disgraced a Bench".*

The stairs have been worn away from use by generations of seamen and rivermen, and some even say that Nelson himself once landed here!

Directions: Enter The Town of Ramsgate

The Town of Ramsgate Public House: This attractive Pub is long and narrow. The wood panelling adds atmosphere, as does the wooden deck which overhangs the Thames and everything is set off with a mock gallows complete with noose.

The Pub was built in the early 1600s and was originally called The Red Cow, apparently after a particular red-headed barmaid! The Pub was later renamed the Town of Ramsgate, due to the Ramsgate fishermen who would sell their fish on the Wapping Old Steps.

It is said that Captain Blood was apprehended in the bar of this Pub in 1671, while hiding from the law. He was wanted after apparently stealing the Crown Jewels and attempting to assassinate King Charles II.

The extensive wine cellars below this Pub were once used as holding cells for men who had been press-ganged by the Admiralty. Naval personnel would prowl the streets at night to force men over the age of twelve years into joining the Royal Navy as sailors. The reward for the captors was £10 for each man (or boy) pressed into service. Many men were easily captured when drunk. The innocent men were held here, in the cellars, as though they were prisoners, before being transported to waiting ships. So, as you can see, visiting the Pubs on this Walk a few centuries ago was fraught with many kinds of dangers.

These cellars were later used to imprison men, women and children, who had been convicted of minor offences. The prisoners would be held in the overcrowded cellars in atrocious conditions, sometimes for months, before being forced onto waiting ships and transported on a one-way voyage to America and, later Australia.

The Pub garden, at the side of the Pub, is a good place to sit and relax on a pleasant day and enjoy the panoramic view of the Thames. Note, however, that this area, now such a pretty garden, was originally used as a place of execution for thieves. On certain days of the month, people were brought here and publicly hung. Crime and punishment in the 1600s! It is no wonder then that the Pub claims that the bar is haunted!

Directions: Exit the Pub and turn right, returning to Wapping Underground Station ❶. We recommend that you do not miss the last Pub on this Walk. To reach the Mayflower Pub, which is directly opposite on the other side of the River Thames, we will need to cross the River by Underground to Rotherhithe Underground Station ❾ using the East London Line on Platform 2. It is only one stop on the Tube and takes only two minutes. Then there is another two-minute walk to The Mayflower Pub.

If you do not have a Daily Underground Pass then ask for a ticket to Rotherhithe Underground Station. A single ticket will cost approximately £0.90p.

Directions: As you exit Rotherhithe Underground Station ❾, turn left and immediately turn first left into Railway Avenue. Continue to the end of the street. Turn left and on the left, the building with a large chimney is the Brunel Engine House ❿

Brunel Engine House: The Thames Tunnel, which links Wapping to Rotherhithe was the first underwater tunnel in the world and was built by Marc Brunel between 1825 and 1843. Today, the Brunel Engine House is a Museum telling the story of Brunel's historical project; it is regarded as one of the most important industrial archaeological sites in London.

Directions: Continue past the Brunel Engine House and immediately on the right, at No. 117 Rotherhithe Street, is The Mayflower Pub ⓫

The Mayflower Public House: This pretty restored 16th century Pub w.. originally called The Spread Eagle and was only renamed The Mayflower i 1957, in honour of its historical past. The Pub commands brilliant views over th Thames and has its own patio, which extends over the River.

In 1618, Captain Christopher Jones, who lived locally, moored his ship - Th Mayflower - at the rear of this tiny Pub. Captain Jones then prepared Th Mayflower for the Pilgrim Fathers. The Pilgrim Fathers were Puritans, who wer under threat of persecution, and so they had decided to take the long an dangerous journey across the Atlantic to the New World, where they intende to build a new colony.

It was from this Pub in 1620 that the Pilgrim Fathers filed along the jetty t board The Mayflower for the first stage of their journey. The Pub claims tha from the Pub patio, you can still see this original jetty.

The Pilgrim Fathers sailed to Southampton, to meet a second ship, Th Speedwell, and then went onto Plymouth, from where they were to begin the historical voyage to America.

The Mayflower finally set sail from Plymouth, England on the 6th Septembe 1620 after two false starts because The Speedwell was taking in water. Durin the arduous voyage to America, only one person died. There were two birth one baby was born at sea and was named Oceanus; the second baby was bor after arrival, and was named Peregrine (meaning "coming from abroad" o "pilgrim").

The Pilgrim Fathers arrived at the coast of New England, at a place they name "Plymouth" on 21st December 1620. This day is today celebrated in America, a Forefathers' Day. During the following four months, in New England, over ha the Pilgrims died from an epidemic of scurvy, pneumonia and tuberculosis.

The Mayflower returned from America, arriving in England in May 162. Despite the terrible hardships, not one of the surviving Pilgrim Fathers returne home with the ship.

The Mayflower continued working for a short while on journeys to Europe, bu after Captain Jones died, here in Rotherhithe, on 5th March 1622, the ship wa